A Look in Time

Carrie Waters

Sadlier-Oxford
A Division of William H. Sadlier, Inc.

Contents

4

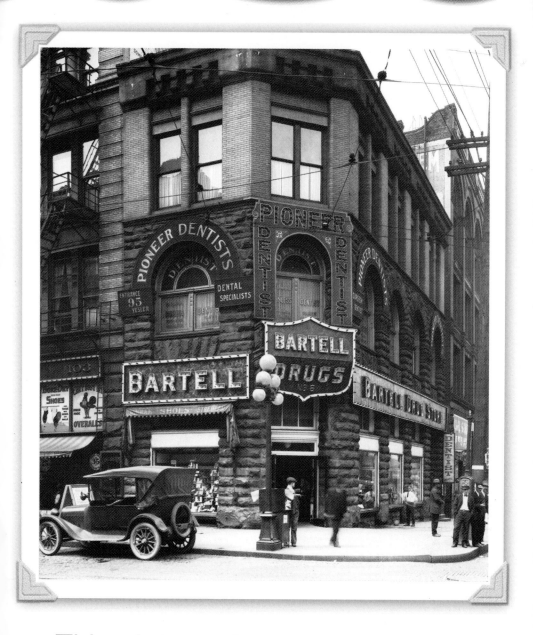

This picture shows a town many years ago. Many things have changed since then.

Stores

Back then, most people got food at small grocery stores like this one. They got bread at bakeries. They got meat at butcher shops.

Today, many people get their food at supermarkets. Supermarkets sell all kinds of food.

Cars

Long ago, people drove cars like this one. See the crank on the front? The driver had to turn it to start the car.

Today, drivers just turn a key to start their cars. Most roads and streets are paved, and cars can go much faster.

Safety

Back then, the town fire truck was a wagon pulled by horses. Firefighters had to get the horses ready to go in a hurry.

Firefighters today still hurry to put out fires. But they ride in trucks with powerful engines and can get to fires much faster.

Schools

Long ago, schools were much smaller. Many had only one or two rooms. Children sat on long benches and wrote on slates.

Today, schools have more
classrooms and more children.
Children sit at tables or desks.
They write on paper or work
on computers.

Homes

This is how a kitchen looked long ago. People kept milk and other foods in large boxes filled with ice. They mixed bread dough and cake batter by hand.

Kitchens look very different today.
People have machines that help
make cooking easier. Refrigerators
keep food cold. Electric mixers
can mix food in seconds.

People

Back then, grown-ups went to work. Children went to school and played with friends. Families like this one had fun together.

Today, grown-ups go to work. Children go to school and play with friends. Families like this one have fun together.

Some things haven't changed at all!

Look what else has changed
from then to now.

Then → **Now**

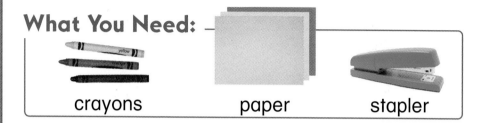
My Social Studies Project

Make a Time Display

What You Need:

crayons   paper   stapler

What You Do:

1. Draw a picture of something people used long ago. Label it.

2. Draw a picture of something people use today. Label it.

3. Draw a picture of something used both long ago and today. Label it.

4. Staple the pictures together to make a three-sided display.

Index